# Festivals through the Year
# Spring

Anita Ganeri

Heinemann
LIBRARY

First published in Great Britain by Heinemann Library
Halley Court, Jordan Hill, Oxford OX2 8EJ
a division of Reed Educational and Professional Publishing Ltd.
Heinemann is a registered trademark of Reed Educational & Professional Publishing Limited.

OXFORD MELBOURNE AUCKLAND IBADAN JOHANNESBURG
BLANTYRE GABORONE PORTSMOUTH (NH) USA CHICAGO

Designed by Ken Vail Graphic Design, Cambridge
Illustrations by Pat Murray
Printed by Wing King Tong in Hong Kong

02 01 00 99
10 9 8 7 6 5 4 3 2

ISBN 0 431 05456 8

**British Library Cataloguing in Publication Data**

Ganeri, Anita
Spring. – (Festivals through the year)
1. Spring festivals – Great Britain – Juvenile literature
I. Title
394.2'62'0941

**Acknowledgements**

The Publishers would like to thank the following for permission to reproduce photographs:
Andes Press Agency, p. 8, (Carlos Reyes Manzo), p. 20; Bridgeman Art Library, pp. 17, 27;
Celtic Picture Library, p. 6; Circa Photo Library/R. Beeche, p. 10; Collections/Jarrold Publishing, p. 12;
Emmett, Phil & Val, p. 22; Greenhill, Sally, p. 16; Harmdee Singh Sagoo, p.24; Jayawardane, Jayasiri,
p. 28; Peerless, Ann & Bury, p. 13; Radovan, Zev, pp. 9, 19; Robert Harding Picture Library/Adam
Woolfitt, p. 4; Sanders, Peter, pp. 14, 15, 26; Slide File, p. 7; Soester, Juliette, p. 18.

Cover photograph reproduced with permission of Slide File

Our thanks to Peter Woodward, who works with SHAP Working Party on World
Religions in Education, for his comments in the preparation of this book.

Every effort has been made to contact copyright holders of any material reproduced in this book.
Any omissions will be rectified in subsequent printings if notice is given to the Publisher.

# Contents

Celebrating spring    4

St David's Day    6

St Patrick's Day    7

Purim    8

Holi    10

Mother's Day    12

Ramnavami    13

Id-ul-Adha    14

April Fool's Day    16

Pesach    17

Easter    20

Baisakhi    24

Al-hijrah    26

St George's Day    27

Wesak    28

Glossary    30

Index    32

Words printed in **bold letters like these** are explained in the Glossary.

# Celebrating spring

After the cold of winter, spring is a joyful time. The weather gets warmer and the days get longer. Nature seems to come back to life. The trees burst into bud and the first flowers bloom. It is a time of new life and celebration.

Many festivals are held in springtime. Some mark the end of winter and welcome in the spring. Many have special religious meanings, when people remember the birthdays of their gods or teachers and important times in their religion's history.

Many baby animals are born in spring.

Festivals are often happy times with many ways of celebrating. There are special services and ceremonies, delicious food, dancing, cards and gifts. Some festivals are holidays when you have a day off school.

Some festivals happen on the same day each year. Others change from year to year. For festivals that change, you will find a dates circle, which tells you when the festival will be. (The future dates of some festivals are only decided upon nearer the time, so some dates in the circles may be out by a day or two.)

Dates

7 April 1998
26 April 1999
15 April 2000
4 April 2001
8 April 2002

## Moon dates

*The calendar we use every day has a year of 365 days, divided into 12 months. Most months have 30 or 31 days. Some religions use different calendars which are based on the Moon. A Moon month is the time it takes for the Moon to travel around the Earth. This is about 27 days, which gives a shorter year. So, each year, the Moon calendar falls out of step with the everyday calendar. This is why some festivals fall on different days each year.*

# St David's Day

On 1 March, Welsh people celebrate St David's Day. St David is the **patron saint** of Wales. According to legend, he was a **Christian monk** who lived hundreds of years ago. He was famous for his **holy** powers. When his teacher went blind, David gave him back his sight.

St David lived with his monks in a **monastery**. It was a very hard life. The monks were not allowed to speak and had only bread, salt and vegetables to eat. David later became **archbishop** of Wales.

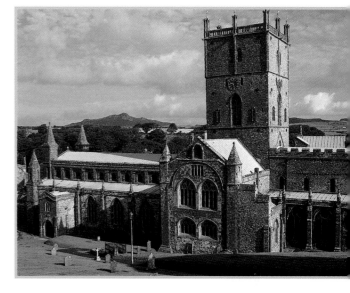

St David's **Cathedral** in Wales.

## Leeks and daffodils

*To celebrate St David's Day, people wear leeks or daffodils pinned to their clothes. The leek is a sign that winter is over. The daffodil is a sign of spring.*

# St Patrick's Day

On 17 March, Irish people celebrate St Patrick's Day. St Patrick is the **patron saint** of Ireland. This is a very jolly day and no one goes to school or work. There are parades through the streets and lots of parties.

Patrick was born in Britain hundreds of years ago. When he was just 16, he was **kidnapped** and taken to Ireland to be sold as a slave. He later escaped and became a **priest**. St Patrick spent his life teaching people about **Christianity**.

These girls are dancing in a St Patrick's Day parade in Dublin.

## Three leaves

On St Patrick's Day, people wear a three-leaved shamrock. St Patrick is said to have used the three leaves to teach people three ways of thinking about God.

# Purim

The **Jewish** festival of Purim is held in February or March. It remembers the **Jews** who lived in Persia more than 2000 years ago. A man called Haman helped the king to rule. He hated the Jews and wanted to have them all killed. The king agreed. But when he realized that his wife, Queen Esther, was Jewish too, the king gave orders for Haman to be killed instead.

## A play for Purim

Purim is a very joyful festival. Children go to fancy dress parties and play tricks on their parents. They also put on plays and act out the story of Purim. You could try doing this with your friends.

At Purim, many Jews go to the **synagogue** to hear the story of Queen Esther. Every time wicked Haman is mentioned, children try to make as much noise as possible. They boo, shout, stamp their feet and shake special rattles, called greggors. All this is done to drown out the sound of Haman's name.

Dates

12 March 1998
2 March 1999
20 March 2000
9 March 2001
26 February 2002

Special three-cornered cakes are eaten at Purim. They are called Hamantaschen, or sometimes Haman's purses. They are made of pastry filled with honey and poppy seeds.

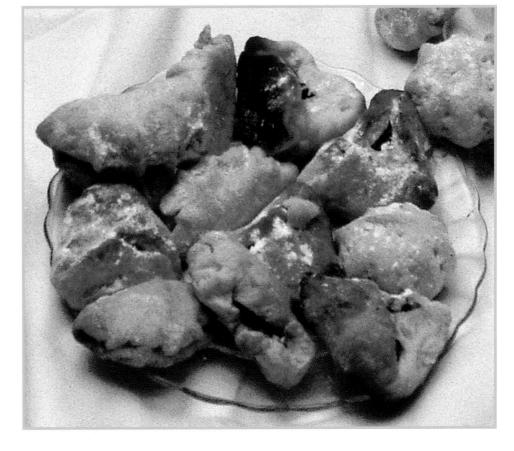

# Holi

Holi is the happiest festival in the **Hindu** year. It is celebrated in February or March. It marks the end of winter and the coming of spring. In India, where Holi began, this was when farmers celebrated the first harvest of the year.

*Dates*

12 March 1998
3 March 1999
21 March 2000
10 March 2001
Later dates not known

It is best to wear your oldest clothes for Holi. You may get covered with brightly coloured water or powder!

On the night before Holi, a big bonfire is built. This reminds people of the wicked witch, Holika, who gave the festival its name. There was once a prince who worshipped the god, **Vishnu**. Holika tried to kill him by burning him in a fire. But Vishnu saw what was happening and rescued the prince from the flames.

Next day, the real fun begins. People play tricks and squirt each other with coloured water. These are like the games that the god, **Krishna**, used to play with his friends. In the evening, people visit their relations with gifts of sweets and wish them happy Holi.

## Roasting coconuts

*In some places, people throw coconuts into the bonfire as offerings to the gods. They leave them to roast, then break them open and eat the sweet insides. They believe that this gives them the gods' blessings.*

# Mother's Day

**Dates**

22 March 1998
14 March 1999
9 April 2000
25 March 2001
10 March 2002

The six weeks before Easter are called Lent. This is a very serious time for **Christians**. They remember the time **Jesus** spent in the desert, **fasting** and thinking about how to do God's work.

Mothering Sunday, or Mother's Day, falls on the fourth Sunday in Lent. On Mother's Day, children give gifts of cards and flowers to their mother to thank her for all the good things she does throughout the year.

Mother's Day service in church.

## Happy Mother's Day!

*Try making your own Mother's Day card. Decorate it with flowers made of card or twists of tissue paper. Stick them on with glue or tiny pieces of double-sided tape. Then write a poem inside.*

# Ramnavami

At Ramnavami in March or April, **Hindus** celebrate the birthday of the god **Rama**. Rama is one of the most popular of all the Hindu gods. He is the hero of the Ramayana, a very long poem which is one of the Hindu **holy** books. It tells the story of Rama and his beautiful wife, Sita, who is **kidnapped** by Ravana, an evil demon king. With the help of the monkey god, Hanuman, Rama finds Sita and rescues her.

On Rama's birthday, Hindus go to the **mandir** to hear the Ramayana being read. They also sing songs of worship and take turns in rocking a cradle with an **image** or picture of Rama inside.

Rama and Sita with their friend, Hanuman the monkey god.

# Id-ul-Adha

Id-ul-Adha is a **Muslim** festival, held at the end of the **Hajj pilgrimage**. This is a special journey to **Makkah** which all Muslims hope to make. Makkah is a city in Saudi Arabia. It is the Muslims' most important **holy** place, because it is where the **Prophet Muhammad (pbuh)** first taught people to follow **Allah**.

*Dates*
7 April 1998
27 March 1999
15 March 2000
7 March 2001
25 February 2002

These Muslims are on the Hajj pilgrimage to Makkah.

Id-ul-Adha is celebrated all over the world. It is the time when Muslims remember the story of **Ibrahim** from the Qur'an, their holy book. Ibrahim was about to kill his son to show how much he loved Allah. Just in time, a voice told him to stop. He killed a goat instead.

Today, at Id-ul-Adha, Muslims kill a sheep or lamb to remind them of Ibrahim's love for Allah. Butchers do this for Muslims in Britain. Some meat is given to friends and relations. Some is given to the poor. People also give each other gifts and cards, and wear new clothes.

Muslims visit the **mosque** for prayers at Id-ul-Adha.

## Five Pillars

The Hajj is one of the Five Pillars of **Islam**. These are five duties Muslims try to carry out:
1 Believing in Allah and Muhammad (pbuh).
2 Praying five times a day.
3 Giving money to the poor.
4 **Fasting** during the holy month of Ramadan.
5 Making the Hajj pilgrimage to Makkah.

# April Fool's Day

On 1 April it is April Fool's Day, a time for playing tricks and practical jokes on your family and friends. You could hide their shoes, or pretend someone wants them on the phone. Anyone who falls for a trick is called an April Fool. It is great fun thinking up new tricks to play. But watch out! If you don't play your trick by midday, you become the Fool instead. And make sure the tricks you play are not dangerous!

No one knows why 1 April was picked for this festival. It might be that now spring has come, everyone wants to have some fun.

April Fool!

## Hunting the Gowk

In Scotland, April Fool's Day is known as Hunt the Gowk. A gowk is a cuckoo or a fool. A trick is called a huntegowk. It must be played before midday or you become the cuckoo.

# Pesach (1)

The **Jewish** festival of Pesach celebrates how God helped the **Jews** escape from Egypt long ago. Their lives were very miserable. They had to work like slaves. A man called **Moses** was chosen by God to lead the Jews to safety. But the king of Egypt sent his army after them. There seemed no way of escape. But God parted the waters of the sea so that the Jews could cross. Then the water flooded back, drowning the Egyptian soldiers.

Dates
11 April 1998
1 April 1999
20 April 2000
8 April 2001
28 March 2002

The parting of the waters.

# Pesach (2)

At Pesach, **Jews** celebrate with a special meal called the **Seder**. As they eat, they tell the story of the first Pesach. The youngest child in the family asks four questions. The first is 'Why is this night different from all other nights?' The other questions are about the food on the table. Each dish has a special meaning.

A Jewish family sitting down for their Seder meal.

Pesach is a serious festival when Jews remember their history. But it is also a happy time for being with your family. Pesach is also called Passover.

## Special foods

*At the Seder meal, Jews eat bitter foods, like **horseradish**, to remind them of how unhappy the Jews were in Egypt. They also eat sweet foods to celebrate their freedom. There is a dish of flat, dry crackers called matzot. The Jews left Egypt in such a hurry, they could not wait for the bread they were baking to rise. Eating matzot reminds them of this.*

*Charoset (a sweet mixture of apples, nuts and wine) – for the cement used by Jews in buildings for their Egyptian masters.*

*Horseradish – has a bitter taste for unhappiness.*

*Parsley – a sign of spring and of hope.*

A dish of *salty water* stands for tears.

*Lamb bone* – for the lambs killed in Egypt and offered to God.

*Hard-boiled egg* – another offering to God.

# Easter

For **Christians**, Easter is a special spring festival. It is when they remember how **Jesus** died on the cross and celebrate how he came back to life again. The story of Easter is told in the Bible, the Christians' **holy** book.

This **church** window shows Jesus on the cross. This is called the Crucifixion.

Jesus went to **Jerusalem** for the Passover (or Pesach) festival. He knew that his life was in danger because his enemies did not like what he taught. He shared a last meal with his followers and then went to a garden to pray. While he was there, soldiers came for him. He was put to death by being nailed to a large wooden cross. Two days later, when his friends visited his tomb, they found it was empty. Jesus had come back to life! They saw him several more times before he went up to heaven.

Jesus's coming back to life is called the Resurrection. Christians believe it shows that death is not something to be afraid of. It is the start of a new life with God.

## The cross

There are crosses in every Christian church. Some Christians wear a cross as a necklace or a badge. The cross reminds them of how Jesus died. This is why people eat hot cross buns at Easter.

# Holy Week

The week before Easter is called **Holy** Week. It was the last week of **Jesus**'s life. It begins with Palm Sunday, when Jesus rode into **Jerusalem** on the back of a donkey. Crowds of people came to cheer, waving palm leaves to welcome him. When **Christians** go to **church** on Palm Sunday, they are given a small palm-leaf cross to remind them of that day.

*Dates*
(Easter Sunday)
12 April 1998
4 April 1999
23 April 2000
15 April 2001
31 March 2002

(Note: In the Orthodox Church, Easter is celebrated on different dates.)

Easter service in church.

Jesus died on Friday. The name Good Friday comes from 'God's Friday'. It also refers to Jesus's goodness, because Jesus was good to give up his life for others. He rose from the dead on Easter Sunday. This is a very happy day. Christians attend special services in church to thank God for Jesus's life.

## Easter eggs

Do you know why people give chocolate eggs at Easter? Eggs stand for new life. They celebrate Jesus's rising from the dead. Eggs also remind us of spring, when many animals have their young.

## Decorating eggs

You could try decorating your own eggs for Easter. First empty an egg by making two holes with a pin, one large and one small, in each end of the egg. Blow through the small hole so the egg comes out of the big hole at the other end into a bowl. Wash and dry the egg. Then you can paint your egg, or cover it with pieces of tissue paper glued in place, or even give it a face and add woollen hair.

# Baisakhi

On 14 April, **Sikhs** celebrate the festival of Baisakhi. This is the start of the Sikh New Year and an important day in Sikh history.

On Baisakhi in 1699, the Sikh leader, **Guru Gobind Singh**, called all the Sikhs together. He asked if any of them would die for their beliefs. Five men stepped forward. But the **Guru** did not kill them. His question was a test. Instead, they became the first members of a special group called the **Khalsa**.

At Baisakhi the special flag which flies outside the **Gurdwara** is taken down and a new one put up in its place.

Today, Sikhs celebrate Baisakhi with services in the Gurdwara. These may last all day. There are readings from the Sikhs' **holy** book, the Guru Granth Sahib, and a special meal to share. This is also the time when many young Sikhs join the Khalsa. Then they count as full members of their religion.

## The Five Ks

*When Sikhs join the Khalsa, they promise to wear five signs of their beliefs. These are called the five Ks.*

1 *Kesh – uncut hair. Sikh men wear a **turban** to keep their long hair tidy.*
2 *Kangha – a comb to look after your hair.*
3 *Kara – a steel bracelet.*
4 *Kirpan – originally a sword, but now often small enough to be worn on the comb under the turban.*
5 *Kaccha – cotton shorts, now usually worn under clothes.*

# Al-hijrah

Dates

27 April 1998
16 April 1999
5 April 2000
26 March 2001
15 March 2002

Al-hijrah is New Year's Day in the **Muslim** calendar. It is the day on which Muslims remember the **hijrah**, a journey which the **Prophet Muhammad (pbuh)** made hundreds of years ago. Muhammad's teachings about **Allah** were unpopular in **Makkah**, where he lived. So he moved to another city, called Madinah. Here many people became his followers.

Al-hijrah means the day of the hijrah. Muslims celebrate by telling stories about Muhammad and saying extra prayers.

This is the Prophet's **Mosque** in Madina the city in which Muhammad settled.

## Muslim calendar

*The hijrah is so important for Muslims that they start their calendar from the date on which it happened. After each year, Muslims write the letters AH which mean 'year of the hijrah'. The year 1999 is 1420 AH.*

# St George's Day

St George's Day is on 23 April. St George is the **patron saint** of England. Legend says that he was a soldier who lived hundreds of years ago. He was famous for his bravery.

Once George met a fearsome, fire-breathing dragon. It had already eaten several children from a nearby town and was about to gobble up the king's daughter. George killed the dragon and rescued the young princess. In return, the townspeople became **Christians**, like George.

St George's **emblem** was a red cross on a white background. It decorated his armour and shield. It is now used as part of the English flag.

On St George's Day, many people wear a red rose. This is the special flower of England.

St George killing the dragon.

# Wesak

The **Buddhist** festival of Wesak happens in April or May. On this day, many Buddhists celebrate three special events: the **Buddha**'s birthday, his enlightenment, and his passing away (death). Enlightenment means suddenly seeing things clearly. It is a bit like turning on the light in a dark room. It means that the Buddha saw the truth about the world. It is this truth that he taught his followers.

A **monk** talking to Buddhist children on Wesak Day.

Wesak is the biggest Buddhist festival. It is also called Buddha Day. Buddhists decorate their homes with lamps and flowers and send Wesak cards to their friends. Then they dress in simple, white clothes and visit the **vihara** to pay their respects to the Buddha. It is a day for being especially kind and generous to others, as the Buddha taught.

### Dates
9 May 1998
30 April 1999
18 May 2000
7 May 2001
Later dates not known

## Jataka stories

At Wesak, children listen to stories about the Buddha. These are called Jataka stories. The Buddha often appears as an animal in the stories to teach an important lesson. In one story, he is a lion whose life is saved by a jackal. Instead of eating the jackal, as a hungry lion would, he lets him go. This teaches the children that one good turn deserves another.

# Glossary

**Allah** – Muslim word for God

**archbishop** – very senior Christian priest

**Buddha** – great teacher who lived about 2500 years ago

**Buddhist** – someone who follows the teachings of the Buddha

**cathedral** – important Christian church, where a bishop (senior priest) is based

**Christian** – person who follows the teachings of Jesus

**Christianity** – religion of the Christians

**church** – Christian place of worship

**emblem** – special symbol or badge

**fasting** – not eating or drinking

**Gurdwara** – Sikh place of worship

**Guru** – Sikh teacher

**Guru Gobind Singh** – Sikh leader who started the Khalsa

**Hajj** – pilgrimage made by Muslims to Makkah

**hijrah** – journey which the Prophet Muhammad (pbuh) made from Makkah to Madinah. It marks the start of the Muslim calendar.

**Hindu** – to do with the Hindu religion which began in India about 4500 years ago. A Hindu is someone who follows the Hindu religion.

**holy** – means respected because it is to do with God

**horseradish** – bitter-tasting plant root, used to make sauce

**Ibrahim** – prophet of Islam who was ready to kill his son to prove his love for Allah

**image** – picture or statue of a god or goddess

**Islam** – religion of the Muslims. It began about 1400 years ago in Saudi Arabia.

**Jerusalem** – city in Israel which is very important for Jews, Christians and Muslims

**Jesus** – religious teacher who lived about 2000 years ago. Christians believe that he was the son of God.

**Jewish** – to do with the Jewish religion

**Jew** – person who follows the Jewish religion, which began in the Middle East more than 4000 years ago

**Khalsa** – the Sikh community, or family. A special ceremony is held for Sikhs joining the Khalsa.

**kidnapped** – taken away against your will

**Krishna** – popular Hindu god, often shown with blue skin. Krishna is famous for playing tricks.

**Makkah** – city in the country we now call Saudi Arabia where the Prophet Muhammad (pbuh) was born. It is the Muslims' holiest place.

**mandir** – Hindu place of worship. Also called a temple.

**monastery** – place where monks live and worship

**monk** – man who gives up his possessions and devotes his life to God. Monks have to obey a strict set of rules.

**Moses** – great Jewish leader who lived about 3500 years ago

**mosque** – Muslim place of worship

**Muhammad** – the last great prophet of Islam. He was chosen by Allah to teach people how to live.

**Muslim** – person who follows the religion of Islam

**patron saint** – saint who looks after a particular country or a particular group of people, such as travellers or doctors

**pbuh** – these letters stand for 'peace be upon him'. Muslims add these words after Muhammad's name and the names of the other prophets.

**pilgrimage** – special journey made to a holy place

**priest** – holy man or religious leader

**prophet** – person chosen by God to be his messenger

**Rama** – popular Hindu god

**Ramadan** – holy month for Muslims when they fast from dawn to sunset every day

**Seder** – special meal eaten at the Jewish festival of Pesach

**Sikh** – person who follows the Sikh religion, which began in India about 500 years ago

**synagogue** – Jewish place of worship

**turban** – long piece of cloth which Sikh men wind around their heads to keep their hair tidy

**vihara** – Buddhist place of worship

**Vishnu** – one of the most important Hindu gods. Vishnu is worshipped as the protector of the world.

# Index

Al-hijrah 26
Allah 14, 15, 26, 30
April Fool's Day 16
archbishops 6, 30
Baisakhi 24–25
Bible 20
Britain 7
Buddha 28, 29, 30
Buddhists 28, 29, 30
cards 5, 12, 15, 29
Christianity 7, 30
Christians 6, 12, 20, 21, 22, 23, 27, 30
churches 20, 22, 30
Crucifixion 20, 21
Easter 20–23
Egypt 17, 19
England 27
fasting 12, 15, 30
food 5, 9, 11, 18, 19, 23
God 12, 17, 23
Good Friday 23
Gurdwaras 25, 30
Gurus 24, 30
Guru Gobind Singh 24, 30
Guru Granth Sahib 25
Hajj 14, 15, 30
Haman 8–9
Hanuman 13
Hindus 10, 13, 30
Holi 10–11
Holy Week 22–23
Ibrahim 15, 30
Id-ul-Adha 14–15
India 10
Ireland 7
Islam 15, 30
Jerusalem 20, 22, 30
Jesus 12, 20, 21, 22, 23, 30
Jews 8, 9, 17, 18, 19, 30
Khalsa 24, 25, 31

Krishna 11, 31
Lent 12
Makkah 14, 15, 26, 31
mandir 13, 31
monasteries 6, 31
monks 6, 28, 31
Moon months 5
Moses 17, 31
mosques 15, 31
Mother's Day 12
Muslim 14, 15, 26, 31
New Years 24, 26
Palm Sunday 22
Passover (see Pesach)
patron saints 6, 7, 27, 31
Pesach 17–20
pilgrimage 14, 15, 31
prayers 15, 26
priests 7, 31
Prophet Muhammad (pbuh) 14, 15, 26, 31
Purim 8–9
Qur'an 15
Rama 13, 31
Ramadan 15, 31
Ramayana 13
Ramnavami 13
St David's Day 6
St George's Day 27
St Patrick's Day 7
Saudi Arabia 14
Scotland 16
Seder 18–19, 31
Sikhs 24, 25, 31
Sita 13
synagogues 9
viharas 29, 31
Vishnu 11
Wales 6
Wesak 28–29